The Power Within: Defeating Negative Self-Talk

Julian Schmidt

Copyright © [2023]

Title: The Power Within: Defeating Negative Self-Talk

Author's: Julian Schmidt.

All rights reserved. No part of this publication may be reproduced, stored in a retrieval system, or transmitted in any form or by any means, electronic, mechanical, photocopying, recording, or otherwise, without the prior written permission of the publisher or author, except in the case of brief quotations embodied in critical reviews and certain other non-commercial uses permitted by copyright law.

This book was printed and published by [Publisher's: Julian Schmidt] in [2023]

ISBN:

TABLE OF CONTENTS

Chapter 1: Understanding Negative Self-Talk
07

What is Negative Self-Talk?

The Impact of Negative Self-Talk on Our Lives

Recognizing Patterns of Negative Self-Talk

Chapter 2: The Origins of Negative Self-Talk
14

Childhood Influences on Negative Self-Talk

Cultural and Societal Influences on Negative Self-Talk

Personal Experiences and Traumas that Contribute to Negative Self-Talk

Chapter 3: The Power of Positive Self-Talk
20

The Benefits of Positive Self-Talk

Techniques for Cultivating Positive Self-Talk

Creating Affirmations to Counter Negative Self-Talk

Chapter 4: Challenging and Reframing Negative Thoughts 26

Identifying Negative Thought Patterns

Cognitive Behavioral Strategies for Challenging Negative Thoughts

Reframing Techniques to Shift Negative Self-Talk to Empowering Self-Talk

Chapter 5: Building Resilience and Self-Compassion 33

Developing Resilience in the Face of Negative Self-Talk

Practicing Self-Compassion and Self-Acceptance

Cultivating a Growth Mindset to Overcome Negative Self-Talk

Chapter 6: Strategies for Overcoming Negative Self-Talk 40

Mindfulness and Meditation Practices

Journaling and Reflection Exercises

Seeking Support and Professional Help

Chapter 7: Maintaining a Positive Mindset and Self-Talk   47

Daily Practices for Nurturing Positive Self-Talk

Surrounding Yourself with Positive Influences

Overcoming Setbacks and Staying Committed to Positive Self-Talk

Chapter 8: Embracing Self-Love and Empowerment   53

The Importance of Self-Love in Overcoming Negative Self-Talk

Cultivating a Sense of Empowerment and Confidence

Integrating Self-Care Practices into Daily Life

Chapter 9: Sustaining Positive Self-Talk for Long-Term Change   59

Creating a Personalized Self-Talk Plan

Overcoming Relapses and Staying Motivated

Celebrating Successes and Embracing a Positive Life Outlook

Chapter 10: The Power Within: Living a Life Free of Negative Self-Talk   65

Embracing the Journey of Self-Transformation

Inspiring Others to Overcome Negative Self-Talk

The Enduring Power of Positive Self-Talk: A Life of Self-Fulfillment and Happiness

Chapter 1: Understanding Negative Self-Talk

What is Negative Self-Talk?

Negative self-talk is the internal dialogue we have with ourselves that is filled with self-criticism, doubt, and pessimism. It is the voice in our head that consistently focuses on our flaws, limitations, and failures. This detrimental habit of negative thinking can have a profound impact on our mental well-being, self-esteem, and overall quality of life.

Negative self-talk often originates from past experiences, societal expectations, and comparison to others. It can take various forms, such as berating ourselves for mistakes, doubting our abilities, and predicting failure before even attempting something. These thoughts are like weeds that slowly suffocate our confidence and prevent us from reaching our full potential.

Everyone is susceptible to negative self-talk, regardless of age, gender, or background. It affects individuals from all walks of life, making it crucial to recognize its presence and take proactive steps to overcome it. The first step is becoming aware of our negative thoughts and acknowledging their impact on our emotions and actions.

Negative self-talk can manifest in different ways, such as generalizations ("I always mess things up"), catastrophizing ("If I fail this test, my life is over"), and personalizing ("They canceled plans with me; it must be because they don't like me"). These thoughts are designed to keep us stuck in a cycle of self-doubt, preventing us from taking risks and pursuing our goals.

It is important to understand that negative self-talk is not based on reality but rather on distorted perceptions and beliefs. Challenging these negative thoughts with evidence and alternative perspectives is crucial to breaking free from their grip. By questioning the validity of our negative self-talk, we can replace it with more positive and empowering thoughts.

Defeating negative self-talk requires practice and persistence. It involves cultivating self-compassion, developing a growth mindset, and surrounding ourselves with positive influences. Learning to reframe our thoughts, focusing on our strengths and accomplishments, and setting realistic expectations are essential steps towards overcoming negative self-talk.

In this book, "The Power Within: Defeating Negative Self-Talk," we will explore various strategies and techniques to help you recognize, challenge, and ultimately conquer negative self-talk. By understanding the impact of our thoughts and actively working towards transforming them, we can unlock our true potential, boost our self-esteem, and live a happier, more fulfilling life. Remember, you have the power within you to silence the negativity and embrace a more positive and empowering mindset.

The Impact of Negative Self-Talk on Our Lives

Introduction:

Negative self-talk is a pervasive habit that affects people from all walks of life. Whether you are a student, a professional, a parent, or anyone else, the power of negative thoughts can have a profound impact on your overall well-being and success. In this subchapter, we will explore the detrimental effects of negative self-talk and how it can hinder personal growth, relationships, and overall happiness. By understanding the consequences of negative self-talk, we can begin to take steps towards defeating it and unleashing the power within us.

1. Self-Limiting Beliefs:

Negative self-talk often stems from self-limiting beliefs that we hold about ourselves. These beliefs can create a vicious cycle of doubt, fear, and self-sabotage. When we constantly tell ourselves that we are not good enough, smart enough, or deserving enough, we hinder our ability to reach our full potential. Our negative thoughts become self-fulfilling prophecies, keeping us stuck in a state of unhappiness and underachievement.

2. Impact on Relationships:

Negative self-talk not only affects our self-perception but also influences how we interact with others. When we constantly put ourselves down, we project negativity onto those around us. This can lead to strained relationships, as our negative thoughts breed insecurity, jealousy, and resentment. By recognizing the impact of negative self-talk on our interactions, we can actively work towards cultivating healthier relationships based on positivity and self-acceptance.

3. Mental and Physical Health:

The impact of negative self-talk extends beyond our emotional well-being. It can take a toll on our mental and physical health as well. Persistent negative thoughts can lead to chronic stress, anxiety, depression, and even physical ailments like headaches and muscle tension. By acknowledging the connection between our thoughts and our overall health, we can prioritize self-care and develop strategies to combat negative self-talk.

4. Breaking Free from Negative Self-Talk:

The first step towards defeating negative self-talk is awareness. By recognizing our negative thought patterns, we can challenge and replace them with positive affirmations. Additionally, surrounding ourselves with a supportive network of friends, family, or professionals can provide the encouragement and guidance needed to break free from the grips of negative self-talk. It is essential to cultivate self-compassion and practice self-care to counteract the damaging effects of negative self-talk.

Conclusion:

Negative self-talk can have a profound impact on our lives, hindering personal growth, damaging relationships, and affecting our mental and physical health. However, by recognizing the detrimental effects of negative thoughts and taking proactive steps towards defeating them, we can unleash the power within us. It is within our control to reframe our self-talk and cultivate a positive mindset that empowers us to live a fulfilling and successful life. Remember, the power to defeat negative self-talk lies within you.

Recognizing Patterns of Negative Self-Talk

Negative self-talk is a common phenomenon that affects almost everyone at some point in their lives. It refers to the inner dialogue we have with ourselves, often filled with self-doubt, criticism, and negativity. These patterns of negative self-talk can be detrimental to our mental well-being and can hinder personal growth and success. However, by recognizing and understanding these patterns, we can take the first step towards defeating them and harnessing the power within us.

One common pattern of negative self-talk is the "catastrophizing" mindset. This happens when we automatically assume the worst-case scenario in every situation, blowing things out of proportion. For example, if we make a small mistake at work, we might convince ourselves that we are going to be fired, leading to heightened anxiety and stress. Recognizing this pattern is essential, as it allows us to challenge these irrational thoughts and replace them with more realistic and positive ones.

Another pattern of negative self-talk is the "personalization" trap. This occurs when we take everything personally, blaming ourselves for situations that are not entirely within our control. For instance, if a friend cancels plans, we might immediately assume that it is because of something we did wrong. By recognizing this pattern, we can remind ourselves that not everything is about us and that people's actions are often influenced by various factors beyond our control.

Additionally, the pattern of "overgeneralization" can greatly impact our self-esteem. This involves making sweeping generalizations based on one negative experience. For example, if we fail at a particular task, we might conclude that we are a failure in all aspects of life. Recognizing this pattern allows us to challenge these extreme beliefs and focus on our strengths and past successes instead.

To recognize these patterns, it is crucial to cultivate self-awareness. Pay attention to your inner dialogue and the emotions that arise as a result. Take note of recurring patterns and themes that emerge, as these offer valuable insights into your negative self-talk tendencies.

By recognizing patterns of negative self-talk, we gain the power to counteract them with positive affirmations and self-compassion. We can challenge our negative thoughts by asking ourselves if there is evidence to support them or if they are purely based on irrational fears and insecurities. By replacing negative thoughts with positive ones, we can gradually rewire our brains to think more positively and foster a healthier mindset.

Remember, everyone experiences negative self-talk from time to time. It is a natural part of being human. However, by recognizing these patterns and actively working to defeat them, we can unleash the power within ourselves and cultivate a more positive and fulfilling life.

Chapter 2: The Origins of Negative Self-Talk

Childhood Influences on Negative Self-Talk

Our childhood experiences play a significant role in shaping our beliefs, attitudes, and behaviors. Unfortunately, for many of us, these early years can also be the breeding ground for negative self-talk. Negative self-talk refers to those internal dialogues filled with self-criticism, doubt, and pessimism that can hinder our progress and overall well-being.

During childhood, we are highly impressionable, and our minds absorb everything around us like sponges. The messages we receive from our parents, teachers, peers, and society at large can have a lasting impact on how we perceive ourselves and the world. If we grew up in an environment where criticism and negativity were prevalent, it is likely that we internalized those messages and developed a pattern of negative self-talk.

Parents who constantly berate their children, belittle their accomplishments, or set unrealistic expectations can unknowingly foster negative self-talk. Similarly, growing up in a school environment where bullying is prevalent or being surrounded by peers who engage in constant comparison can also contribute to the development of negative self-talk.

Furthermore, traumatic experiences during childhood, such as abuse, neglect, or witnessing violence, can profoundly affect a child's self-worth and lead to negative self-talk. These experiences create deep-rooted beliefs that they are unworthy, unlovable, or inadequate, perpetuating a negative cycle of thoughts.

Recognizing the childhood influences on negative self-talk is the first step towards breaking free from its grip. Understanding that these negative thoughts are not a true reflection of our worth or capabilities is crucial. It is important to challenge these beliefs and replace them with positive affirmations and self-compassion.

Healing childhood wounds requires self-reflection, self-awareness, and sometimes seeking professional help. By addressing the root causes of our negative self-talk, we can begin to rewrite the narrative and cultivate a more positive mindset.

Remember, negative self-talk is not a permanent state. It is a learned behavior that can be unlearned. Through self-care, self-acceptance, and surrounding ourselves with positive influences, we can gradually shift our mindset and develop a healthier relationship with ourselves.

In conclusion, childhood influences play a significant role in shaping our self-perception and internal dialogue. Negative self-talk often stems from experiences and messages received during our formative years. Recognizing these influences and actively working towards healing and self-compassion is essential in breaking free from the grip of negative self-talk. Remember, you have the power within to defeat negative self-talk and create a more positive and empowering mindset.

Cultural and Societal Influences on Negative Self-Talk

In our modern world, negative self-talk has become a pervasive issue that affects individuals from all walks of life. Whether you are a student, a professional, a parent, or a retiree, negative thoughts can infiltrate your mind and hinder your personal growth and happiness. However, it is important to recognize that these negative thoughts are not solely a result of our internal struggles. In fact, cultural and societal influences play a significant role in shaping and perpetuating this destructive pattern of self-talk.

One major cultural influence on negative self-talk is the media. In today's society, we are bombarded with images of perfection and success. From social media platforms to television shows, we are constantly exposed to carefully curated versions of people's lives, often highlighting only their achievements and positive experiences. This constant comparison to an unrealistic standard can lead to feelings of inadequacy and self-doubt, fueling negative self-talk. It is crucial to remind ourselves that these portrayals are often far from reality and that everyone has their own unique struggles and imperfections.

Furthermore, societal expectations and pressures can also contribute to negative self-talk. Society often places great emphasis on external factors such as appearance, wealth, and status. This constant pressure to meet these expectations can lead to self-criticism and a sense of never being good enough. It is important to challenge these societal norms and redefine success and happiness on our own terms. By focusing on our personal growth, values, and achievements, we can break free from the cycle of negative self-talk.

Additionally, cultural upbringing and family dynamics can greatly influence our self-perception and inner dialogue. Negative self-talk can be learned from a young age through critical parenting or cultural beliefs that emphasize self-criticism as a form of motivation. Recognizing these influences and actively working towards self-compassion and self-acceptance is crucial for breaking free from negative self-talk patterns.

In conclusion, negative self-talk is not solely an internal struggle but is heavily influenced by cultural and societal factors. By understanding these influences, we can begin to challenge and overcome the destructive patterns of self-doubt and self-criticism. It is important to cultivate self-compassion, redefine success on our own terms, and surround ourselves with positive influences that promote self-growth and acceptance. Remember, you have the power within to defeat negative self-talk and embrace a more positive and fulfilling mindset.

Personal Experiences and Traumas that Contribute to Negative Self-Talk

Negative self-talk, the persistent and critical inner voice that undermines our self-esteem and confidence, is an issue that affects countless individuals across all walks of life. Whether you are a student, professional, parent, or simply someone dealing with the everyday challenges of existence, negative self-talk can take a toll on your mental well-being and hinder your personal growth. To truly understand and combat this destructive cycle, it is crucial to explore the personal experiences and traumas that often contribute to its development.

Everyone has experienced moments in life that have left them feeling vulnerable, hurt, or inadequate. These experiences can range from childhood bullying to toxic relationships, from failures and rejections to traumatic events. Each of these encounters has the potential to shape our perception of ourselves and influence the way we talk to ourselves internally.

For instance, imagine a student who constantly received criticism and belittlement from their parents, teachers, or peers. Over time, these negative messages become internalized, leading to a diminished sense of self-worth and a tendency to engage in self-sabotaging thoughts. Similarly, individuals who have faced traumatic events, such as abuse or accidents, may develop a negative self-image due to the blame or shame they associate with those experiences.

Furthermore, societal pressures and media influence can exacerbate negative self-talk. We live in a world that idolizes certain beauty standards, achievements, and lifestyles, leaving many feeling inadequate and unworthy. Comparing ourselves to others and constantly falling short can contribute to a vicious cycle of negative self-talk.

It is important to recognize that these personal experiences and traumas are not definitive sentences that determine our self-worth. They do not define us, but they can shape our perspectives and affect the way we talk to ourselves. Understanding the origins of our negative self-talk is the first step towards reclaiming our power and defeating its grip on our lives.

In the forthcoming chapters, we will delve deeper into strategies and techniques to combat negative self-talk. By addressing the root causes and challenging the validity of our negative thoughts, we can begin to reframe our internal dialogue and foster a more positive and empowering mindset.

Remember, you are not alone in this struggle. Negative self-talk knows no boundaries and affects people from all walks of life. Together, we can navigate the path towards self-acceptance, self-love, and personal growth.

Chapter 3: The Power of Positive Self-Talk

The Benefits of Positive Self-Talk

In today's fast-paced and demanding world, it is all too easy to fall prey to negative thoughts and self-doubt. Countless individuals find themselves trapped in a cycle of negative self-talk, which can have detrimental effects on their overall well-being. However, the power to break free from this destructive pattern lies within each and every one of us. By embracing the benefits of positive self-talk, we can transform our mindset and unlock our true potential.

Negative thoughts have a way of seeping into every aspect of our lives. They can erode our confidence, hinder our progress, and limit our ability to achieve our goals. Thankfully, positive self-talk can act as a powerful antidote to counteract these harmful patterns. By consciously replacing negative thoughts with positive affirmations, we can rewire our brain to focus on our strengths, accomplishments, and potential.

One of the key benefits of positive self-talk is its ability to boost self-confidence. When we consistently remind ourselves of our capabilities and worth, we begin to believe in ourselves and our abilities. This newfound confidence empowers us to take on challenges, overcome obstacles, and reach new heights in both our personal and professional lives.

Furthermore, positive self-talk has a profound effect on our mental and emotional well-being. By shifting our mindset to focus on gratitude, resilience, and self-compassion, we can reduce stress, anxiety, and depression. Instead of dwelling on past failures or worrying about the future, positive self-talk helps us stay present and appreciate the beauty of each moment.

In addition to improving our mental health, positive self-talk also enhances our physical well-being. Research has shown that individuals who engage in positive self-talk experience lower blood pressure, reduced risk of heart disease, and improved immune system function. By cultivating a positive mindset, we can strengthen our body's ability to heal and thrive.

Harnessing the benefits of positive self-talk is not always easy, especially if negative thoughts have become deeply ingrained. It requires commitment, practice, and patience. However, with time and effort, we can rewire our brain to automatically default to positive self-talk, ultimately transforming our lives for the better.

In conclusion, positive self-talk is a powerful tool that can help us break free from the grip of negative thoughts. By embracing the benefits of positive self-talk, we can boost our self-confidence, improve our mental and emotional well-being, and enhance our physical health. It is within each and every one of us to harness the power within and defeat negative self-talk. Start today and witness the incredible transformation that positive self-talk can bring to your life.

Techniques for Cultivating Positive Self-Talk

Negative thoughts can be incredibly debilitating and can prevent us from achieving our full potential. They have the power to chip away at our self-esteem, hinder progress, and create a cycle of self-doubt. However, by cultivating positive self-talk, we can break free from this destructive pattern and unlock the power within us. In this subchapter, we will explore various techniques to help you develop positive self-talk and conquer negative thoughts.

1. Awareness: The first step towards change is recognizing negative self-talk patterns. Pay attention to your inner dialogue and identify any negative thoughts that arise. Awareness is key to interrupting negative patterns and replacing them with positive ones.

2. Reframing: Challenge negative thoughts by reframing them. Replace self-defeating statements with empowering ones. For example, if you catch yourself thinking, "I can't do this," reframe it as, "I am capable of overcoming any challenge."

3. Affirmations: Utilize positive affirmations to rewire your brain. Create a list of affirmations that resonate with you and repeat them daily. Examples include, "I am worthy of love and success," or "I am confident and capable."

4. Visualization: Visualize yourself succeeding and achieving your goals. Create a mental image of the positive outcome you desire. Visualizing success can help you build confidence and overcome self-doubt.

5. Gratitude: Cultivate gratitude for the positive aspects of your life. Focus on what you have rather than what you lack. Gratitude shifts your mindset towards positivity and helps counter negative thoughts.

6. Surround yourself with positivity: Surround yourself with people who uplift and support you. Engage in activities that bring you joy and fill your life with positivity. This will create an environment that fosters positive self-talk.

7. Self-compassion: Treat yourself with kindness and compassion. Replace self-criticism with self-acceptance. Understand that everyone makes mistakes, and it is through these mistakes that we learn and grow.

8. Practice mindfulness: Be present in the moment and observe your thoughts without judgment. Mindfulness helps you detach from negative thoughts and prevents them from controlling your emotions.

Remember, cultivating positive self-talk is a journey that requires patience and persistence. Celebrate small victories along the way and be gentle with yourself during setbacks. By implementing these techniques, you can gradually transform your negative self-talk into a powerful tool for personal growth and success. Embrace the power within you to defeat negative self-talk and unlock your true potential. You deserve it.

Creating Affirmations to Counter Negative Self-Talk

Negative self-talk can be incredibly damaging to our well-being and overall happiness. It is a common struggle that affects people from all walks of life. Whether you constantly doubt your abilities, criticize yourself harshly, or let fear and self-doubt control your actions, negative self-talk can hold you back from reaching your full potential.

Fortunately, there is a powerful tool that can help you combat these negative thoughts and replace them with positive ones – affirmations. Affirmations are positive statements that you can repeat to yourself daily, helping to rewire your thought patterns and replace negative self-talk with empowering beliefs.

To create your own affirmations, it is important to follow a few key steps. First, identify the negative thoughts that plague your mind the most. These could be statements like "I'm not good enough," "I always fail," or "I'll never be successful." Once you have identified these negative beliefs, you can start crafting affirmations to counter them.

When creating affirmations, focus on using positive language and framing your statements as if they have already come true. For example, instead of saying "I am not a failure," rephrase it to "I am successful in all that I do." By using present tense and positive language, you are training your mind to believe these statements to be true.

Make your affirmations specific to your personal goals and desires. If you want to boost your self-confidence, create affirmations like "I am confident and capable in all areas of my life." If you are working towards a promotion at work, affirmations like "I am deserving of success and will achieve my professional goals" can be powerful.

Consistency is key when it comes to affirmations. Repeat them daily, multiple times a day if possible. Write them down, say them out loud, or even record them and listen to them during your daily routine. The more you repeat these positive statements, the more they will become ingrained in your subconscious mind, replacing the negative self-talk that has held you back.

Remember, creating affirmations is a personal process. Take the time to reflect on your own negative thoughts and tailor your affirmations to counter them directly. With consistent practice, you will start to notice a shift in your mindset and a reduction in negative self-talk. Embrace the power within you to create positive change and overcome the limitations of negative thoughts.

Chapter 4: Challenging and Reframing Negative Thoughts

Identifying Negative Thought Patterns

In our daily lives, we often find ourselves grappling with negative thoughts that can hinder our progress and happiness. These negative thought patterns can have a significant impact on our overall well-being and prevent us from reaching our full potential. However, by learning to identify and overcome these patterns, we can reclaim our power and cultivate a more positive mindset. In this subchapter, we will explore the various negative thought patterns that frequently plague us and delve into strategies to defeat them.

Negative thought patterns can manifest in different ways and affect various aspects of our lives. They can stem from self-doubt, fear of failure, past traumas, or societal pressures. Some common negative thought patterns include self-criticism, catastrophic thinking, overgeneralization, and mind-reading. Understanding these patterns is crucial to breaking free from their grip.

Self-criticism is often the harshest and most damaging negative thought pattern. It involves constantly berating ourselves for perceived flaws and mistakes, leading to a decrease in self-esteem and confidence. Catastrophic thinking, on the other hand, involves always anticipating the worst possible outcome in any given situation, leading to anxiety and unnecessary stress.

Overgeneralization is a pattern where we draw sweeping conclusions based on limited experiences. For instance, if we fail at something once, we might conclude that we will never succeed at anything, which can severely limit our potential. Mind-reading, another common negative thought pattern, involves assuming we know what others are thinking about us, often assuming the worst, which can lead to feelings of insecurity and isolation.

To overcome negative thought patterns, we must first become aware of them. Mindfulness and self-reflection play a crucial role in this process. Paying attention to our thoughts and emotions can help us identify recurring negative patterns and recognize the triggers that set them off. Journaling, meditation, or seeking professional help are effective tools to delve deeper into our negative thought patterns and gain insights into their origins.

Once we have identified these patterns, we can challenge and reframe them. This involves questioning the validity of our negative thoughts and replacing them with more positive and realistic alternatives. For example, if we catch ourselves engaging in self-criticism, we can consciously remind ourselves of our strengths and achievements. By consistently practicing this positive self-talk, we can gradually rewire our thinking patterns.

In conclusion, negative thought patterns can be detrimental to our well-being, but identifying and overcoming them is within our power. By becoming aware of these patterns and utilizing various strategies to challenge and reframe them, we can take control of our thoughts and cultivate a more positive mindset. Remember, the power to defeat negative self-talk lies within each one of us.

Cognitive Behavioral Strategies for Challenging Negative Thoughts

Introduction:

In our daily lives, we often find ourselves battling negative thoughts that weigh us down and hold us back from reaching our full potential. These negative thoughts can come in various forms, such as self-doubt, fear, or even a persistent feeling of unworthiness. However, by understanding and implementing cognitive behavioral strategies, we can effectively challenge and overcome these negative thoughts, paving the way for a more positive and fulfilling life.

1. Recognize and Identify Negative Thoughts: The first step in challenging negative thoughts is to become aware of their presence. Pay attention to the thoughts that run through your mind and identify those that are negative or self-deprecating. By acknowledging their existence, you can begin to take control of them.

2. Evaluate the Evidence: Negative thoughts often arise from distorted thinking patterns. Challenge these thoughts by examining the evidence behind them. Ask yourself: Is there any solid proof to support this negative thought? Often, you will find that there is lack of evidence or that the evidence is based on assumptions rather than facts.

3. Reframe and Replace Negative Thoughts: Once you have identified the negative thoughts and evaluated their validity, it is time to reframe them into more realistic and positive ones. Replace negative thoughts with more accurate, encouraging, and compassionate statements. For example, if you find yourself thinking,

"I will never succeed," reframe it to, "I am capable of achieving my goals with determination and effort."

4. Practice Positive Self-Talk:
Positive self-talk plays a significant role in challenging negative thoughts. Engage in positive affirmations and statements that reinforce your self-worth, capabilities, and potential. Repeat these statements daily, and gradually, you will begin to believe and internalize them.

5. Challenge Cognitive Distortions:
Cognitive distortions are thinking patterns that contribute to negative thoughts. Common distortions include overgeneralization, jumping to conclusions, and all-or-nothing thinking. Learn to recognize and challenge these distortions. Ask yourself if there is another perspective or alternative explanation to the situation at hand.

6. Seek Support:
Don't hesitate to seek support from friends, family, or professionals when challenging negative thoughts becomes overwhelming. Surround yourself with positive influences and individuals who believe in your potential. Their encouragement and guidance can provide the necessary motivation and perspective.

Conclusion:
Challenging negative thoughts is an ongoing process that requires practice and patience. By implementing cognitive behavioral strategies, you can gradually shift your mindset from one dominated by negativity to a more positive and empowering one. Remember, you

have the power within you to defeat negative self-talk and create a fulfilling life filled with self-belief and positivity.

Reframing Techniques to Shift Negative Self-Talk to Empowering Self-Talk

Introduction:

In our daily lives, we often find ourselves engaged in negative self-talk. These thoughts can be toxic and detrimental to our overall well-being. However, with the right techniques, we can reframe our negative self-talk into empowering and positive self-talk. In this subchapter, we will explore various reframing techniques that will help you defeat negative self-talk and harness the power within yourself.

1. Identify and Challenge Negative Thoughts:

The first step towards reframing negative self-talk is to become aware of our negative thoughts. Pay attention to the language you use when talking to yourself. Once you identify a negative thought, challenge its validity. Ask yourself, "Is this thought based on facts or assumptions?" By questioning the negative thoughts, you allow yourself to gain a different perspective and shift towards a more empowering mindset.

2. Replace Negative Statements with Positive Affirmations:

Negative self-talk often involves statements like "I can't," "I'm not good enough," or "I always fail." Challenge these statements and replace them with positive affirmations. For example, instead of saying "I can't do it," reframe it as "I am capable of overcoming any challenge." By consciously replacing negative statements with positive affirmations, you rewire your brain to focus on solutions rather than limitations.

3. Use Visualization Techniques:

Visualization is a powerful tool to combat negative self-talk. When you find yourself engaged in negative thoughts, close your eyes and visualize a positive outcome. Visualize yourself succeeding, being confident, and achieving your goals. This technique helps to shift your focus from self-doubt to empowerment, enabling you to take action towards your aspirations.

4. Practice Gratitude:

Gratitude is a transformative practice that can shift your mindset from negativity to positivity. Take a few minutes each day to reflect on things you are grateful for. By acknowledging the positive aspects of your life, you redirect your thoughts towards empowerment and abundance.

5. Surround Yourself with Positive Influences:

The people we surround ourselves with greatly impact our self-talk. Surround yourself with positive, supportive individuals who uplift and inspire you. Engage in activities that bring you joy and boost your self-esteem. By surrounding yourself with positive influences, you create an environment that fosters empowering self-talk.

Conclusion:

Reframing negative self-talk into empowering self-talk is a journey that requires commitment and practice. By utilizing these techniques, you can gradually shift your mindset from negativity to empowerment. Remember, you have the power within you to defeat negative self-talk and unleash your true potential. Embrace the power of reframing, and watch as your life transforms for the better.

Chapter 5: Building Resilience and Self-Compassion

Developing Resilience in the Face of Negative Self-Talk

Introduction:

In our fast-paced and constantly evolving world, negative self-talk has become an all too common occurrence. We often find ourselves bombarded with thoughts that undermine our self-worth, hinder our progress, and create a barrier to personal growth. However, it is essential to remember that we possess the power within us to conquer these negative thoughts and develop resilience. This subchapter aims to provide practical strategies to help individuals from all walks of life overcome negative self-talk and cultivate a resilient mindset.

Understanding Negative Self-Talk:

Negative self-talk can manifest in various ways, such as self-criticism, self-doubt, and a constant focus on perceived inadequacies. It is crucial to recognize that these thoughts are not a reflection of our true potential but rather a result of conditioning and external influences. Acknowledging this fact is the first step towards developing resilience.

Challenging Negative Self-Talk:

To develop resilience, we must challenge the negative thoughts that plague our minds. One effective technique is to question the validity of these thoughts. Ask yourself, "Is this thought based on facts or assumptions?" Often, you will find that these thoughts are irrational and have no basis in reality. Replacing negative thoughts with positive affirmations can also help rewire our thinking patterns and build resilience.

Cultivating a Growth Mindset:

A growth mindset is the belief that our abilities can be developed through dedication and hard work. Embracing this mindset allows us to view setbacks and failures as opportunities for growth and learning. By reframing negative self-talk as a call for improvement, we empower ourselves to bounce back stronger and cultivate resilience.

Practicing Self-Compassion:

Self-compassion is the key to developing resilience in the face of negative self-talk. Treat yourself with the same kindness, understanding, and support you would offer a loved one facing a similar situation. Accept that everyone has flaws and makes mistakes. By accepting ourselves as imperfect beings, we can break free from the cycle of negative self-talk and develop resilience.

Seeking Support:

Remember that you are not alone in your struggle against negative self-talk. Reach out to trusted friends, family, or professionals who can provide guidance and support. Share your experiences and learn from others who have overcome similar challenges. Surrounding yourself with positive influences can help reinforce resilience and break free from negative thought patterns.

Conclusion:

Developing resilience in the face of negative self-talk is a journey that requires consistent effort and self-reflection. By challenging negative thoughts, cultivating a growth mindset, practicing self-compassion, and seeking support, we can gradually break free from the shackles of negativity and become resilient individuals. Remember, the power to defeat negative self-talk lies within you, waiting to be unleashed. Embrace this power, and unlock your true potential.

Practicing Self-Compassion and Self-Acceptance

In a world filled with constant comparison and judgment, it is crucial to develop self-compassion and self-acceptance as powerful tools to combat negative thoughts. We all experience moments of self-doubt and criticism, but it is how we respond to these thoughts that truly matters. This subchapter aims to guide you on a journey towards embracing yourself with kindness and embracing your flaws with acceptance.

Self-compassion begins with recognizing that you are human and that making mistakes is a natural part of life. Instead of berating yourself for perceived failures, try offering yourself the same compassion and understanding you would give to a dear friend. Treat yourself with kindness, speak to yourself with gentle words, and acknowledge that everyone has their own unique struggles.

Accepting yourself fully is another integral component of defeating negative self-talk. Embrace your strengths, but also acknowledge your weaknesses without judgment. Remember that no one is perfect, and it is our imperfections that make us beautifully human. Instead of striving for an unattainable ideal, focus on personal growth and progress.

Practicing self-compassion and self-acceptance involves cultivating a mindset of gratitude. Take a moment each day to appreciate your accomplishments, big or small, and give yourself credit for the effort you put into various aspects of your life. Recognize that you are deserving of love, care, and happiness, just like anyone else.

It is also essential to challenge the negative beliefs that often fuel negative self-talk. Replace self-criticism with positive affirmations and realistic self-appraisal. Recognize the strengths and qualities that make you unique, and celebrate them. Surround yourself with a supportive network of friends and family who uplift and encourage you, helping to counteract any negative thoughts that may arise.

Remember that self-compassion and self-acceptance are ongoing practices. Be patient with yourself as you navigate this journey, and don't expect immediate results. Gradually, you will notice a shift in your mindset and an increased sense of self-worth as you learn to embrace yourself fully.

In conclusion, practicing self-compassion and self-acceptance is vital for overcoming negative thoughts. By treating yourself with kindness, embracing your flaws, and challenging negative beliefs, you can cultivate a positive mindset and defeat negative self-talk. Remember, you are worthy of love, happiness, and acceptance, just as you are.

Cultivating a Growth Mindset to Overcome Negative Self-Talk

Negative self-talk is something that affects almost everyone at some point in their lives. It is that nagging voice inside our heads that tells us we are not good enough, smart enough, or capable enough to achieve our goals and dreams. It can be debilitating and can hinder our personal and professional growth. However, by cultivating a growth mindset, we can overcome negative self-talk and unlock our true potential.

A growth mindset is the belief that our abilities and intelligence can be developed through dedication and hard work. It is the understanding that failure and setbacks are opportunities for learning and growth, rather than indications of our inherent limitations. By adopting a growth mindset, we shift our perspective from a fixed mindset, where we believe our abilities are fixed and unchangeable, to a mindset that embraces challenges, perseveres through obstacles, and thrives on continuous improvement.

To cultivate a growth mindset, it is essential to become aware of our negative self-talk patterns. Pay attention to the thoughts that arise when faced with challenges or setbacks. Are they self-defeating and discouraging, or do they foster resilience and determination? By recognizing negative self-talk, we can challenge and reframe these thoughts into more positive and empowering ones.

One effective way to overcome negative self-talk is through the power of positive affirmations. Affirmations are statements that reinforce positive beliefs about ourselves and our abilities. By repeating affirmations such as "I am capable of achieving my goals" or "I am resilient and can overcome any obstacle," we reprogram our subconscious mind to embrace a growth mindset and reject negative self-talk.

Another powerful tool in cultivating a growth mindset is embracing a love for learning. Instead of viewing failure as a personal flaw, see it as an opportunity to learn and grow. Seek out new challenges and push yourself beyond your comfort zone. Embrace feedback and use it as a tool for improvement rather than criticism.

Surrounding yourself with a supportive network of like-minded individuals can also have a significant impact on overcoming negative self-talk. Seek out mentors, coaches, or friends who believe in your potential and challenge you to grow. Engage in positive self-talk and encourage others to adopt a growth mindset as well.

In summary, cultivating a growth mindset is crucial for overcoming negative self-talk and unlocking our true potential. By becoming aware of our negative self-talk patterns, using positive affirmations, embracing a love for learning, and surrounding ourselves with a supportive network, we can break free from the self-imposed limitations and achieve greatness. Remember, the power to defeat negative self-talk lies within ourselves, and with a growth mindset, we can conquer any negative thoughts that hold us back from living the life we truly desire.

Chapter 6: Strategies for Overcoming Negative Self-Talk

Mindfulness and Meditation Practices

Title: Mindfulness and Meditation Practices: Harnessing the Power Within to Defeat Negative Thoughts

Introduction:
In today's fast-paced world, it is all too easy to get caught up in the whirlwind of negative thoughts that plague our minds. However, by cultivating mindfulness and incorporating meditation practices into our daily routine, we can tap into the power within us and overcome the grip of negative self-talk. This subchapter delves into the transformative potential of mindfulness and meditation, offering valuable tools to combat negative thoughts and embrace a more positive and empowered mindset.

The Power of Mindfulness:
Mindfulness is the practice of bringing one's attention to the present moment, without judgment. By observing our thoughts and emotions without getting entangled in them, we can gain a deeper understanding of our negative patterns and start to rewire our thinking. This subchapter explores various mindfulness techniques, such as breath awareness, body scans, and focused attention exercises, illuminating how they can help us break free from the clutches of negative self-talk.

Meditation Practices for Inner Peace:
Meditation is a powerful tool to cultivate inner peace and silence the

noise of negative thoughts. Through regular practice, we can create a space within ourselves where negative self-talk loses its power. This subchapter introduces different meditation techniques, such as loving-kindness meditation, mantra meditation, and mindfulness meditation, explaining how each practice can guide us towards a calmer and more positive state of mind.

Transforming Negative Thoughts:
Negative thoughts often arise from deep-rooted beliefs and conditioning that limit our potential. This subchapter provides insights into identifying and challenging these negative thought patterns. By combining mindfulness and meditation, we can develop the ability to observe our thoughts objectively and replace negative ones with positive affirmations. Through these practices, we can reframe our mindset, boost self-confidence, and foster a greater sense of self-worth.

Daily Integration and Long-Term Benefits:
The key to harnessing the power of mindfulness and meditation lies in consistent practice and integration into our daily lives. This subchapter offers practical tips on incorporating these practices into our routines, be it through dedicated meditation sessions, mindful eating, or even mindful movement. By creating a sustainable habit, we can experience long-term benefits such as reduced stress, improved focus, increased self-awareness, and enhanced overall well-being.

Conclusion:
In the battle against negative self-talk, mindfulness and meditation practices are powerful allies. By cultivating a deep understanding of our thoughts and emotions, challenging negative thought patterns,

and embracing the present moment, we can tap into our inner power and defeat the grip of negativity. Whether you are new to these practices or already have some experience, this subchapter will guide you on a transformative journey towards a more positive and empowered mindset.

Journaling and Reflection Exercises

In the battle against negative thoughts, one of the most powerful tools at our disposal is journaling and reflection exercises. These exercises provide an outlet for self-expression, self-reflection, and self-discovery. They allow us to examine our negative thoughts and beliefs, challenge them, and ultimately, replace them with more positive and empowering ones. Regardless of who you are or where you come from, journaling and reflection exercises can be beneficial for everyone.

Journaling is a simple yet effective practice that involves putting our thoughts and feelings on paper. By writing down our negative thoughts, we gain a new perspective on them. We can analyze their origins, patterns, and triggers. Through this process, we can identify the underlying causes of our negative self-talk, whether it be past experiences, societal pressures, or personal insecurities. Journaling allows us to externalize our negative thoughts, making them tangible and easier to confront.

In addition to journaling, reflection exercises help us dig deeper into our subconscious mind. These exercises encourage us to ponder on questions such as, "What are the underlying beliefs that contribute to my negative thoughts?" or "What evidence do I have to support these negative beliefs?" By reflecting on these questions, we gain insight into the faulty thought patterns that fuel our negative self-talk. This awareness is the first step towards dismantling and replacing these negative beliefs with more positive and empowering ones.

Furthermore, journaling and reflection exercises also provide an opportunity to celebrate our victories, big or small. By reflecting on moments when we successfully challenged our negative thoughts, we reinforce the idea that we are capable of overcoming them. This builds resilience and confidence in our ability to defeat negative self-talk.

It is important to note that journaling and reflection exercises are personal and unique to each individual. There is no right or wrong way to approach these exercises. Some may prefer to write in a traditional journal, while others might find solace in digital platforms or even voice recordings. The key is to find a method that resonates with you and allows you to express yourself freely.

In conclusion, journaling and reflection exercises are indispensable tools in the battle against negative self-talk. They enable us to externalize our negative thoughts, gain insight into their origins, and challenge the faulty beliefs that underpin them. By incorporating these exercises into our daily routine, we can cultivate a more positive and empowering mindset. So, grab your pen and paper, or your preferred method of expression, and start harnessing the power within through journaling and reflection.

Seeking Support and Professional Help

In our journey to overcome the shackles of negative self-talk, seeking support and professional help becomes an essential step. We are not alone in this battle; there are resources and individuals available to guide us towards a path of self-discovery and empowerment. This subchapter aims to shed light on the importance of reaching out for assistance and the benefits it can bring.

No matter who you are, negative thoughts can affect all aspects of your life. They can cloud your judgment, hinder your progress, and prevent you from achieving your true potential. Recognizing the need for support is the first courageous step towards breaking free from this cycle.

Support can come in various forms. It could be seeking advice from a trusted friend or family member, joining a support group, or even finding solace in online communities dedicated to personal growth. Engaging with like-minded individuals who understand your struggles can provide a sense of belonging and reassurance that you are not alone in your battle against negative self-talk.

In addition to seeking support from peers, professional help plays a crucial role in our journey towards defeating negative thoughts. Consider reaching out to a therapist or counselor who specializes in cognitive-behavioral therapy (CBT). CBT is a proven method that helps individuals identify and challenge their negative thinking patterns, replacing them with healthier and more positive thoughts.

Therapists can provide a safe and non-judgmental space for you to explore the root causes of your negative self-talk. Through their guidance, you can uncover underlying issues, past traumas, or learned behaviors that contribute to your negative mindset. They will equip you with practical strategies and techniques to reframe your thoughts and build resilience against negativity.

Remember, seeking support and professional help is not a sign of weakness, but rather an act of strength and self-care. It demonstrates your commitment to personal growth and your determination to reclaim control over your own mind.

As you embark on this journey, understand that progress may not happen overnight. It requires patience, dedication, and a willingness to confront your inner demons. Embrace the support and professional help available to you, for they will serve as guiding lights illuminating your path towards a brighter, more positive future.

In conclusion, seeking support and professional help is a vital step in conquering negative self-talk. It provides the necessary tools, guidance, and encouragement needed to break free from the chains of negativity. Remember, you are not alone in this battle, and there are resources available to help you unlock the power within and create a life filled with positivity and self-belief.

Chapter 7: Maintaining a Positive Mindset and Self-Talk

Daily Practices for Nurturing Positive Self-Talk

In our daily lives, we encounter various challenges and obstacles that can often lead to negative thoughts and self-talk. These negative thoughts can have a detrimental impact on our overall well-being and hinder our ability to reach our full potential. However, by implementing daily practices for nurturing positive self-talk, we can break free from the chains of negative thinking and empower ourselves to lead happier, more fulfilling lives.

1. Start with self-awareness: The first step in nurturing positive self-talk is to become aware of your negative thoughts. Pay attention to your inner dialogue and identify any recurring negative patterns. By acknowledging these thoughts, you can begin to challenge and replace them with positive affirmations.

2. Practice gratitude: Cultivating a gratitude practice is a powerful way to shift your focus from negativity to positivity. Take a few moments each day to reflect on the things you are grateful for, whether it's the support of loved ones, a beautiful sunset, or a small accomplishment. This practice helps rewire your brain to naturally lean towards positive thoughts.

3. Affirmations and positive self-talk: Create a list of affirmations that resonate with you and repeat them to yourself daily. These positive statements can counteract negative self-talk and help reprogram your

mind for success. For instance, if you catch yourself thinking, "I'm not good enough," replace it with "I am capable and deserving of success."

4. Surround yourself with positivity: Surrounding yourself with positive influences can have a profound impact on your self-talk. Seek out supportive and uplifting individuals who can help you stay on track with your positive thinking journey. Additionally, expose yourself to positive content such as motivational books, podcasts, or inspiring music.

5. Take care of your physical health: Engaging in regular exercise, eating a balanced diet, and getting enough sleep are all essential for maintaining a positive mindset. When your body feels good, it becomes easier to cultivate positive self-talk.

6. Practice mindfulness and meditation: Mindfulness and meditation can help you become more aware of your thoughts and detach from negative thinking patterns. Set aside time each day to practice deep breathing exercises and focus on the present moment. This practice can help quiet the mind and create space for positive self-talk.

Remember, nurturing positive self-talk is a journey, and it requires consistent effort and practice. By implementing these daily practices, you can gradually transform your negative thoughts into empowering and uplifting ones. Embrace the power within you and defeat negative self-talk, unlocking a world of possibilities and personal growth.

Surrounding Yourself with Positive Influences

In a world filled with negativity, it is crucial to protect ourselves from the harmful effects of negative influences. Our thoughts and beliefs shape our reality, and it is essential to cultivate a positive mindset to lead a fulfilling life. The subchapter "Surrounding Yourself with Positive Influences" delves into the importance of surrounding oneself with uplifting and supportive people, as well as creating an environment that fosters positivity.

Negative thoughts can be incredibly damaging, affecting our self-esteem, motivation, and overall well-being. However, by consciously seeking out positive influences, we can counteract those negative thoughts and transform our lives. It is said that we are the average of the five people we spend the most time with. Therefore, it is crucial to evaluate our relationships and make conscious choices about who we allow into our inner circle.

Building a support network of positive influences can be done in various ways. Seeking out like-minded individuals who share similar goals and aspirations can be a great starting point. Engaging in activities such as joining clubs, attending workshops, or participating in community events can help connect with people who have a positive outlook on life. Surrounding yourself with individuals who believe in your potential and support your dreams can be incredibly empowering.

Additionally, it is important to create an environment that nurtures positivity. This can involve decluttering your physical space, organizing your surroundings, and incorporating elements that bring joy and inspiration into your life. Surrounding yourself with uplifting quotes, motivational books, and art that speaks to your soul can have a profound impact on your mindset.

Moreover, it is vital to be mindful of the media we consume. Limiting exposure to negative news, social media toxicity, and other sources of negativity can help protect our mental well-being. Instead, we can choose to consume content that educates, inspires, and uplifts us.

Surrounding ourselves with positive influences can be a powerful tool in defeating negative self-talk. By consciously curating our environment and surrounding ourselves with supportive individuals, we create a foundation for personal growth and self-improvement. Remember, we have the power to choose who and what we allow into our lives. Embrace positivity, and watch as it transforms your thoughts, beliefs, and ultimately your life.

Overcoming Setbacks and Staying Committed to Positive Self-Talk

In our journey towards personal growth and self-improvement, setbacks are inevitable. Life throws curveballs, and negative thoughts can easily creep into our minds, discouraging us from moving forward. However, it is during these challenging moments that our commitment to positive self-talk becomes even more crucial.

Negative thoughts are like weeds that can quickly overtake the garden of our minds. They can drain our energy, erode our self-confidence, and hinder our progress. That's why it is essential to develop strategies to overcome setbacks and stay committed to positive self-talk.

First and foremost, it's crucial to acknowledge that setbacks are a natural part of life. Everyone faces obstacles and experiences failure at some point. Rather than allowing setbacks to define us, we should see them as opportunities for growth and learning. By embracing a growth mindset, we can reframe setbacks as stepping stones towards success.

When faced with a setback, it's essential to practice self-compassion and avoid self-blame. Negative thoughts often arise from the belief that we are not good enough or capable of overcoming challenges. However, by offering ourselves kindness and understanding, we can break free from the cycle of negative self-talk. Treat setbacks as valuable lessons and remind yourself that you are always evolving and improving.

To maintain commitment to positive self-talk, it is helpful to surround yourself with a support system. Seek out like-minded individuals who understand the power of positive thinking and can offer encouragement during difficult times. Sharing your setbacks and challenges with others can provide a fresh perspective and help you regain focus on your journey towards defeating negative self-talk.

Additionally, practicing mindfulness can greatly assist in overcoming setbacks. Mindfulness involves being fully present in the current moment, observing our thoughts and emotions without judgment. By doing so, we can detach ourselves from negative thoughts and redirect our focus towards positive affirmations and self-talk.

Remember that setbacks do not define you; it is how you respond to them that matters. By staying committed to positive self-talk, you can transform setbacks into opportunities for growth and ensure that negative thoughts do not hinder your progress. Embrace a growth mindset, practice self-compassion, seek support, and cultivate mindfulness to overcome setbacks and unleash the power within you.

Chapter 8: Embracing Self-Love and Empowerment

The Importance of Self-Love in Overcoming Negative Self-Talk

Introduction:
Negative self-talk can be a crippling force that holds us back from reaching our true potential. It is a constant barrage of disempowering thoughts and beliefs that can drain our self-confidence and hinder our personal growth. However, there is a powerful antidote to this destructive pattern – self-love. In this subchapter, we will explore the immense importance of self-love in overcoming negative self-talk and how it can transform our lives.

Body:

1.   Understanding Negative Self-Talk:
Negative self-talk is the internal dialogue we have with ourselves, often filled with self-doubt, criticism, and fear. It can stem from past experiences, societal pressures, or even comparing ourselves to others. Recognizing this negative self-talk is the first step towards overcoming it.

2.   The Link Between Self-Love and Self-Talk:
Self-love is the foundation upon which we build a positive self-image. By cultivating self-love, we develop a greater sense of compassion, acceptance, and forgiveness towards ourselves. This, in turn, helps us challenge and reframe our negative self-talk.

3.   Reshaping Our Inner Dialogue:
Self-love allows us to recognize that negative self-talk is not a reflection of our true worth. With self-love as our guide, we can consciously

replace self-sabotaging thoughts with positive affirmations, empowering beliefs, and supportive self-talk.

4. Building Resilience and Confidence:
When we love ourselves, we become resilient in the face of negativity. Self-love helps us bounce back from setbacks, embrace failures as learning opportunities, and believe in our ability to overcome challenges. It fuels our confidence and allows us to pursue our dreams fearlessly.

5. Nurturing a Positive Mindset:
Self-love encourages us to surround ourselves with positivity. By practicing self-care, setting healthy boundaries, and seeking supportive relationships, we create an environment that fosters self-belief and minimizes negative self-talk.

6. Embracing Imperfections:
Self-love teaches us to accept our flaws and imperfections as part of our unique journey. It allows us to let go of unrealistic expectations and embrace self-compassion. By valuing ourselves despite our shortcomings, we can silence the negative self-talk that stems from self-criticism.

Conclusion:
In the battle against negative self-talk, self-love is our most powerful weapon. It empowers us to challenge our inner critic, reshape our thoughts, and ultimately transform our lives. By embracing self-love, we can break free from the chains of negativity and step into a future filled with self-belief, confidence, and personal growth. Remember, you are deserving of love and kindness – starting with yourself.

Cultivating a Sense of Empowerment and Confidence

In today's fast-paced and competitive world, negative thoughts can easily take hold of our minds, hindering our progress and preventing us from reaching our full potential. However, it is essential to understand that we have the power within us to defeat these negative self-talk patterns and cultivate a sense of empowerment and confidence.

Empowerment is the key to unlocking our true potential and overcoming the barriers of negative thoughts. It is about recognizing that we have control over our own lives and that we possess the strength to make positive changes. One of the first steps towards cultivating a sense of empowerment is to identify and challenge the negative thoughts that hold us back.

Negative thoughts can often stem from fear, self-doubt, or past experiences. By examining these thoughts, we can begin to understand their origins and question their validity. Are these negative thoughts based on facts or just assumptions? Are they helping us grow or hindering our progress? By challenging these thoughts, we can start to reframe them into more positive and empowering beliefs.

Building confidence is another crucial aspect of defeating negative self-talk. Confidence is not something we are born with; rather, it is a skill that we can develop over time. One way to boost our confidence is by setting achievable goals and celebrating our successes along the way. Each small victory acts as a stepping stone towards building a stronger belief in ourselves and our abilities.

Surrounding ourselves with supportive and positive influences is also vital in cultivating a sense of empowerment and confidence. Negative self-talk often thrives in environments that lack encouragement and support. By seeking out mentors, friends, or communities that uplift and motivate us, we create a space where positive affirmations can flourish, drowning out the negative voices in our minds.

Furthermore, practicing self-care and self-compassion plays a significant role in empowering ourselves. Taking care of our physical and mental well-being through exercise, healthy eating, and mindfulness techniques can help us build resilience and strengthen our confidence. Additionally, being kind and forgiving towards ourselves when setbacks occur is crucial. Remember that nobody is perfect, and setbacks are merely opportunities for growth and learning.

In conclusion, cultivating a sense of empowerment and confidence is essential for overcoming negative thoughts and reaching our full potential. By challenging negative beliefs, setting achievable goals, surrounding ourselves with positive influences, and practicing self-care, we can develop the power within to defeat negative self-talk and live a more fulfilling and empowered life. Remember, you have the strength to conquer your negative thoughts and become the best version of yourself.

Integrating Self-Care Practices into Daily Life

In our fast-paced world filled with constant pressures, it's crucial to prioritize self-care practices to combat the negative thoughts that often plague our minds. Taking care of ourselves not only enhances our overall well-being but also empowers us to defeat negative self-talk and cultivate a positive mindset. This subchapter will guide you on how to seamlessly integrate self-care practices into your daily routine, regardless of who you are or what niche you belong to.

1. Start with small steps: Incorporating self-care practices may seem overwhelming at first, so begin by incorporating small steps into your daily routine. It could be as simple as setting aside 10 minutes each morning for meditation or enjoying a leisurely walk during your lunch break.

2. Prioritize physical health: Physical well-being plays a significant role in maintaining mental and emotional balance. Engage in regular exercise, nourish your body with healthy meals, and ensure you get enough sleep. These practices will boost your energy levels, improve focus, and help combat negative thoughts.

3. Cultivate mindfulness: Negative thoughts often stem from dwelling on the past or worrying about the future. Practice mindfulness by focusing on the present moment. Engage in activities such as deep breathing exercises, journaling, or practicing gratitude. These practices will help you stay grounded and develop a positive outlook.

4. Create a self-care routine: Designate specific times during the day for self-care activities that bring you joy and relaxation. It could be reading a book, taking a soothing bath, or indulging in a hobby. By

consciously setting aside time for yourself, you'll create a habit of self-care that becomes an integral part of your daily life.

5. Seek support: Surround yourself with a supportive network of family, friends, or like-minded individuals who understand the challenges of negative thoughts. Share your struggles and successes with them, and encourage each other on your journey towards defeating negative self-talk.

Remember, integrating self-care practices into your daily life is an ongoing process. Be patient with yourself and embrace the journey. By prioritizing self-care, you'll gradually transform your thinking patterns and develop a resilient mindset that can overcome any negative self-talk. Start today, and unleash the power within you to defeat negativity and embrace a fulfilling life.

Chapter 9: Sustaining Positive Self-Talk for Long-Term Change

Creating a Personalized Self-Talk Plan

In our journey through life, we often find ourselves plagued by negative thoughts. These thoughts, if left unchecked, can have a detrimental impact on our self-esteem, personal relationships, and overall well-being. However, by developing a personalized self-talk plan, we can begin to regain control over our thoughts and harness the power within us to defeat negative self-talk.

The first step in creating a personalized self-talk plan is to become aware of the negative thoughts that plague our minds. Take a moment to reflect on the common negative thoughts that arise throughout your day. Are they centered around feelings of unworthiness, self-doubt, or fear of failure? Identifying these negative patterns is crucial in order to challenge and replace them with positive and empowering thoughts.

Once you have identified your negative thought patterns, it's time to challenge them. Ask yourself, "Is this thought based on reality or is it just a product of my own insecurities?" Often, negative thoughts are rooted in irrational fears and limiting beliefs. By questioning their validity, you can begin to break free from their grip.

Now that you have challenged your negative thoughts, it's time to replace them with positive and empowering self-talk. Create a list of affirmations and mantras that resonate with you. These can be simple statements like, "I am worthy of love and success" or "I have the power to overcome any obstacle." Repeat these affirmations to yourself throughout the day, especially when negative thoughts arise. Over time, these positive statements will begin to replace the negative self-talk that once controlled your mind.

In addition to affirmations, visualization techniques can also be incredibly powerful in creating a personalized self-talk plan. Take a few moments each day to visualize yourself succeeding, achieving your goals, and living a life free from negative thoughts. Visualization helps to rewire your brain, reinforcing positive beliefs and diminishing the power of negative self-talk.

Finally, surround yourself with a support system of positive and uplifting individuals. Share your self-talk plan with trusted friends or family members who can provide encouragement and hold you accountable. Sometimes, all it takes is a kind and supportive word from someone else to help us break free from negative thought patterns.

Remember, creating a personalized self-talk plan is an ongoing process. It requires patience, commitment, and a willingness to challenge the negative thoughts that have held you back. By taking control of your self-talk, you have the power to transform your life and defeat negative thoughts once and for all.

Overcoming Relapses and Staying Motivated

We all face moments when negative thoughts and self-doubt try to creep back into our lives. It's crucial to recognize that relapses are a common part of the journey towards defeating negative self-talk. However, it's equally important to equip ourselves with the tools and strategies to overcome these setbacks and stay motivated on our path to a positive mindset.

One of the first steps in overcoming relapses is to acknowledge and accept that they are normal. Everyone experiences moments of self-doubt, even the most successful individuals. Understanding this can help us avoid falling into a cycle of self-blame and frustration. Instead, we can focus our energy on finding effective solutions.

One powerful technique is to reframe negative thoughts into positive ones. When a negative thought arises, identify it and challenge its validity. Ask yourself if there is evidence to support this thought or if it's merely a product of your insecurities. Then, consciously replace it with a positive affirmation or belief. For example, if you catch yourself thinking, "I will never succeed," replace it with "I am capable of achieving greatness."

Maintaining a strong support system is also crucial in overcoming relapses and staying motivated. Surround yourself with positive and like-minded individuals who uplift and encourage you. Share your struggles with them and allow them to offer their perspective and support. Additionally, consider seeking professional help, such as therapy or coaching, to gain further guidance and techniques to overcome negative thinking patterns.

Another effective strategy is practicing self-care. Take time to engage in activities that bring you joy and relaxation. Engaging in hobbies or exercise can help distract your mind from negative thoughts and provide a sense of accomplishment. Prioritizing self-care will not only boost your mood but also increase your resilience against relapses.

Setting realistic goals and celebrating small victories is essential to stay motivated. Break down your bigger aspirations into smaller, attainable steps. Celebrate each milestone you reach, as this will reinforce positive thinking and provide momentum to keep going.

Lastly, remember that setbacks are temporary and do not define your worth or capabilities. Embrace failure as an opportunity for growth and learning. Reflect on what you can do differently next time and use setbacks as motivation to come back stronger.

In conclusion, overcoming relapses and staying motivated is an ongoing process that requires self-awareness, support, and effective strategies. By reframing negative thoughts, maintaining a strong support system, practicing self-care, setting realistic goals, and embracing setbacks, you can defeat negative self-talk and cultivate a positive mindset. Remember, your power lies within you, and you have the ability to overcome any obstacle that stands in your way.

Celebrating Successes and Embracing a Positive Life Outlook

In a world full of negative thoughts and self-talk, it is crucial for every individual to celebrate their successes and adopt a positive life outlook. This subchapter aims to guide you towards recognizing your accomplishments, overcoming self-doubt, and embracing a mindset that fosters happiness and success.

We often find ourselves dwelling on our failures or shortcomings, allowing negative thoughts to consume our minds. However, it is important to remember that success comes in all shapes and sizes. Whether it is completing a project at work, taking small steps towards personal growth, or simply getting through a difficult day, every achievement should be celebrated. By acknowledging and appreciating these victories, we can boost our self-esteem and cultivate a positive mindset.

One effective way to celebrate successes is by practicing self-reflection. Take a moment to reflect on your achievements, big or small, and analyze the positive impact they have had on your life. This self-reflection helps in shifting your focus from negative thoughts to your own capabilities and strengths. Additionally, it is essential to surround yourself with a supportive network of friends, family, or mentors who can share in your celebrations and offer encouragement during challenging times.

Overcoming negative self-talk requires a conscious effort to reframe our thoughts. Instead of succumbing to self-doubt and criticism, we must challenge those negative beliefs and replace them with positive affirmations. By acknowledging our worth and potential, we can cultivate a positive life outlook that enables us to take risks, pursue our dreams, and face adversity head-on.

Embracing a positive life outlook goes beyond celebrating successes; it is a continuous practice of gratitude and mindfulness. By focusing on the present moment and appreciating the blessings in our lives, we can shift our perspective from negativity to positivity. Engaging in activities such as journaling, meditation, or practicing acts of kindness can help foster this positive outlook and promote a sense of fulfillment.

In conclusion, celebrating successes and embracing a positive life outlook are crucial steps in defeating negative self-talk. By recognizing our accomplishments, surrounding ourselves with a supportive network, reframing negative thoughts, and practicing gratitude, we can cultivate a mindset that encourages happiness and success. Remember, every individual has the power within to overcome negative thoughts and live a fulfilling life. Start celebrating your successes today and embrace the positive life that awaits you.

Chapter 10: The Power Within: Living a Life Free of Negative Self-Talk

Embracing the Journey of Self-Transformation

In our journey through life, we often find ourselves battling with negative thoughts and self-talk. These negative patterns can hold us back, feeding into feelings of self-doubt, anxiety, and even depression. However, there is a way to break free from this cycle and embrace a transformative journey towards self-empowerment and personal growth.

The key to overcoming negative thoughts lies within ourselves. It is about recognizing that we have the power to change our mindset and reshape our reality. This subchapter, "Embracing the Journey of Self-Transformation," delves into the transformative process of shifting our perspective, cultivating self-compassion, and fostering a positive mindset.

The first step towards self-transformation is acknowledging the negative thoughts that plague our minds. By becoming aware of these patterns, we can begin to challenge and reframe them. This process requires introspection and self-reflection, as we delve deeper into the root causes of our negative self-talk.

Once we have identified these negative thoughts, it is crucial to replace them with positive affirmations and empowering beliefs. This subchapter provides practical exercises and techniques to help readers rewire their minds and replace negative self-talk with empowering statements. These exercises range from visualization techniques to the power of gratitude, helping to shift our focus from what is lacking to what is abundant in our lives.

Moreover, embracing self-transformation involves cultivating self-compassion. It is crucial to recognize that we are all human and prone to making mistakes. By practicing self-compassion, we can forgive ourselves for past failures and embrace a growth mindset. This subchapter explores various self-compassion exercises and strategies to help readers embrace self-forgiveness and let go of self-judgment.

Lastly, this subchapter emphasizes the importance of perseverance and patience in the journey of self-transformation. Change takes time, and setbacks are inevitable. However, by adopting a resilient mindset, we can navigate through these challenges and continue to grow.

"Embracing the Journey of Self-Transformation" is a powerful subchapter that offers valuable insights and practical tools to overcome negative thoughts and embrace personal growth. It is a reminder that we have the power within us to change our lives and create a reality filled with positivity, self-compassion, and empowerment. Whether you are struggling with self-doubt, anxiety, or negative self-talk, this subchapter will guide you on a transformative journey towards a happier, more fulfilling life.

Inspiring Others to Overcome Negative Self-Talk

Subchapter: Inspiring Others to Overcome Negative Self-Talk

Introduction:
In this subchapter, we will delve into the powerful ways in which we can inspire others to overcome negative self-talk. Negative thoughts can be crippling, affecting our self-esteem, relationships, and overall quality of life. However, by understanding the impact of our words and actions, we can become catalysts for change, helping those around us break free from the shackles of self-doubt and negativity.

1. Lead by Example:
One of the most effective ways to inspire others is by leading through our own actions. By modeling positive self-talk and demonstrating a growth mindset, we can show people that it is indeed possible to overcome negative thoughts. Share your personal experiences and highlight the strategies you have used to combat negativity, encouraging others to follow suit.

2. Be Empathetic:
To inspire others, we must first understand their struggles and emotions. Show empathy and validate their feelings, letting them know that they are not alone in their battle against negative self-talk. Be a compassionate listener and offer support without judgment. By creating a safe space, you can inspire them to open up and seek guidance.

3. Share Success Stories:
Human beings are inherently inspired by stories of triumph. Share success stories of individuals who have managed to conquer their

negative self-talk. Highlight the journey they undertook, the obstacles they overcame, and the lessons they learned along the way. These stories can serve as beacons of hope, motivating others to believe in their own ability to overcome negative thoughts.

4. Provide Tools and Strategies:
Equip others with practical tools and strategies that they can implement in their daily lives. Techniques such as positive affirmations, gratitude practices, and cognitive reframing can be powerful tools in combating negative self-talk. Encourage individuals to incorporate these techniques into their routines and guide them through the process if needed.

5. Foster a Supportive Environment:
Create a supportive environment where individuals feel encouraged and empowered to challenge their negative self-talk. Encourage positivity and celebrate small victories along the way. By surrounding themselves with like-minded individuals who are also on a journey of self-improvement, people can draw strength and inspiration from one another.

Conclusion:
Inspiring others to overcome negative self-talk is a transformative act of kindness. By leading through example, showing empathy, sharing success stories, providing tools and strategies, and fostering a supportive environment, we can help individuals break free from the chains of negativity. Remember, every positive change starts with a single step, and by inspiring others, we can contribute to building a community that uplifts and supports one another on the path to self-discovery and growth.

The Enduring Power of Positive Self-Talk: A Life of Self-Fulfillment and Happiness

In our fast-paced and often chaotic world, it's easy to become overwhelmed by negative thoughts. These thoughts can weigh us down, affecting our self-esteem, confidence, and overall happiness. However, there is a powerful tool we all possess that can help us combat these destructive thoughts: positive self-talk.

Positive self-talk is the act of consciously replacing negative thoughts with empowering and uplifting ones. It may seem simple, but its effects can be profound. By changing the way we speak to ourselves, we can transform our mindset, leading to a life of self-fulfillment and happiness.

Negative thoughts have a sneaky way of creeping into our minds, whispering doubts and insecurities. They tell us we're not good enough, that we'll never achieve our goals, or that we don't deserve happiness. But what if we challenged these thoughts? What if we refused to let them control us?

Positive self-talk allows us to do just that. It enables us to reframe our thoughts and beliefs, replacing negativity with positivity. Instead of focusing on our flaws, we can recognize our strengths and abilities. Rather than dwelling on past failures, we can learn from them and use them as stepping stones to success. Positive self-talk empowers us to see setbacks as temporary hurdles, not insurmountable roadblocks.

The enduring power of positive self-talk lies in its ability to shape our reality. When we consistently affirm our strengths, our mind begins to believe them. We become more confident, more resilient, and more capable of achieving our goals. Positive self-talk unlocks our potential, allowing us to tap into the power within.

But positive self-talk is not just about changing our inner dialogue; it's about transforming our external experiences too. When we radiate positivity, we attract positive people and opportunities into our lives. We become magnets for success, as our newfound optimism and self-belief inspire others and open doors previously unseen.

So, how can you harness the enduring power of positive self-talk? Start by becoming aware of your negative thoughts. Challenge them and replace them with positive affirmations. Surround yourself with supportive and like-minded individuals who believe in your potential. Practice gratitude daily, focusing on the blessings in your life. And most importantly, be patient and kind to yourself throughout the journey.

Every one of us has the capacity to defeat negative self-talk and embrace a life of self-fulfillment and happiness. By harnessing the enduring power of positive self-talk, we can transform our thoughts, our beliefs, and ultimately, our lives. It's time to unlock the power within and embrace the incredible possibilities that await us.

www.ingramcontent.com/pod-product-compliance
Lightning Source LLC
LaVergne TN
LVHW052003060526
838201LV00059B/3809